Nightmares & Daydreams

Nightmares & Daydreams

Poems, Thoughts and Meditations
by Portia D.

Liberated Expression
www.liberatedexpression.com
Copyright © 2021 Portia D. Taylor
ISBN: 978-1-949430-00-4
All rights reserved

At a Glance

Olivia.

Home	Pg.3
Army of One	Pg.4-5
(But) I Forgive	Pg.6
Daddy Dearest	Pg. 7-8
Ode to What…	Pg.9-10
R04**	Pg. 11
Truth Is	Pg.12
More Than This	Pg.13
I'm Not a Kid…	Pg. 14
No Love	Pg.15
Mrcme	Pg.16
Forgiveness	Pg.17

Reign.

Killing Me Softly…	Pg.21-22
Them vs. Me	Pg. 23
T.Mac	Pg.24
Just My Type	Pg. 25
Eyes Wide Shut	Pg.26
Bbygirl.P	Pg.27-28
Secret Lovers	Pg.28
This Love Is	Pg.29
Torn and Scorned	Pg.30
Resistance	Pg.31
Find Yourself	Pg.32
Not for Nun	Pg.33-34
[distant] Admiration	Pg.35
[not so] Invincible	Pg.36
Adulting…	Pg.37
Me vs. Them	Pg. 38
[un] Clouded Thought	Pg.39
Self-Love.	Pg.40
Reflect.	Pg.49

Sloane.

Whskeemepls.	Pg.45
Sweet Tooth.	Pg.46-47
Baby Bye.	Pg.48
Computer Love	Pg.49
Bottom of My Glass	Pg.50
Candid Conversations	Pg.51
Damsel.	Pg.52
[don't] Text Me.	Pg.53
All 2018	Pg.54
Every Once in a While.	Pg.55
Us Together	Pg.56
Only with You	Pg.57
But Tonight.	Pg.58
Release.	Pg.59
Wishful Thinking.	Pg.60
Do You?	Pg.61
Spare Me.	Pg.62
Ready.	Pg.63

[Looking for Better]	Pg.64
Balance is	Pg.65
The Jones is Gone	Pg.66
Circa Spring 2016	Pg.67
Strongest Drug…	Pg.68-69
Clouded Thought	Pg.70
Aaand Cut.	Pg.71
Doubt.	Pg.72
When Did I…?	Pg.73
Taxicab Confessions	Pg.74-75
Taxicab Conversations	Pg.76-77
New People.	Pg.78
Clouded Thought.	Pg.79
Love Yourself.	Pg.80
Meet the Author	Pg.81
Gratitude	Pg. 82

This book is dedicated to the most important people in my life: my mom, my dad, my brother and my Nana. I love each of you with everything that I am.

Olivia.

Home.

Where are you?

Not Carbondale, not Chicago or anywhere in between.

Within me I guess, because it's where the heart is, right?

Or where the hurts lies, maybe?

Home is where the pain lingered, where the pain still lingers.

Home is where the anger flourished,

where the hate turned into rage.

No physical structure, but walls of fuck you's,

floors of bitches crying, windows of black eyes,

and doors that welcomed smiling faces –

that didn't know they were walking into a thriving hell.

Army of One for Love.

I wonder does He know what's happening deep down.

Underneath it all, can He see past the complicated and tainted emotions?

They have built these walls that not even I knew were here.

If I had to guess somewhere in the late nineties they began to surface.

The foundation being an absentee father and struggling mother.

Life after that quickly formed a structure so tough, I would wonder

if I'm supposed to be crippled by

the mishaps of my merciless surroundings?

What I need to know is that

He sees this isn't really me.

Does He know that if it were me

I would choose to trust,

I would choose to love,

and I would choose to forgive.

I would never feel the need to be an army of one to protect my love.

I'd never expect the worst and I would know how to accept the good.

Does He see that my heart wants to love with no boundaries?

That love comes effortlessly for me, and everything else takes hard work.

Do you know that I am tired of being strong,

but afraid of being weak?

It's unfamiliar territory.

What if I get caught in the crossfire of my actions and his words?

That would leave me exactly where I am afraid to be, barred and scarred.

Wouldn't even have the strength to revive myself if I tried.

God do you really hear my heart's cries?

(But) I Forgive You...

I vividly remember all the times you should have been, but

You weren't there.

All the times you put on that hideous mask, scaring us.

You thought it was funny.

We sat in the back seat crying out of fear.

Tear after helpless tear.

Not one of them could make it stop.

We just wanted it to stop.

Black kids, blue hearts.

Red eyes, blood shot.

To this day I color my words envy green, because every kid next to me got the family that I could have only dreamed.

Daddy Dearest

What do you call the man that created your life, just to ruin it? – dad, you call that man dad.

He took all his frustrations from his dad out on your mom, and

once the dust settled, you realize he half assed his way through life.

Pretending not to be bitter.

 Pretending the lemonade, he's been gulping is sweet.

Pretending not to be weak, but he reeks of his dad's half ass existence.

So much so that he's basically dead to me,

now.

Some days you go visit, sit and talk for a

while.

Some days you want to call, but you can't.

See the dead only reach out in dreams.

So, subconsciously you're always asleep.

Don't wake me. I'm waiting on my dad to come whisper the sweetest nothings about how things would be if he were still here,

how he's so proud of me, and how I'll always be his baby girl.

How he'd give me the world if he could.

Well dad you could have, or

you could have at least tried, put up a fight.

It was an option, but

You chose yourself over me.

Something like what he did to you.

Ode to What Should Have Been...

[daddy]

I wish you were here to know me...

To hold me

To show me

To uplift me.

I wish you could have told me that they

don't care.

I wish you knew the difference between,

How I cry due to pain, and

When I cry cause beauty hurts, or

when I cry because he and I didn't work.

What about when I laugh?

How it sounds when I'm purposely trying to annoy you, or

When it's too loud for everyone else, or

When it's not genuine, but I don't want to hurt your feelings.

I wish you were here to show me how to work the dance floor.

To escort me to that dance every year,

It's so special—

Even for girls like me.

I wish you were here to try to comb my hair, and

To make me change my clothes because puberty hit,

And suddenly nothing fits, like it did before.

I needed you –

To be my first love, my first trust.

Instead, you were my first heartbreak.

But I need you, still.

A lot of days I'm on the cusp of

Letting you go or letting my heart draw closer.

Every. Single. Thing. reminds me of what wasn't, but –

what should have been.

R04***

Some days I wonder what I'm doing, pursuing this man who brought life,

And tried its end.

The more I know, the more I don't know.

Is this right? – am I living a fairytale lie?

The whirlwind of events left me full of questions, and empty at the same time.

Empty from the lack of understanding.

Empty from the forward thrusts through this rut that he left me in.

Full of good intentions, but still on the bad side of decisions.

Empty from the anguish of the truth.

Full of why and random parked car cries.

They don't cease, and time actually hasn't eased this pain I feel.

Questions with no answers.

Life itself was different after that day.

More different than I could comprehend.

More different than I can comprehend.

That day I was six,

At school after hours, worried. My life has been in a hurry ever since, and deep down I'm hurrying to its end.

Truth Is...

There's no way to make up for the lost time.

We can't rewind it or try again.

There aren't enough thirty-minute conversations from now until our end to,

sever the ties of what should have been.

Forgiveness knew me before I could even process that,

it was you that my heart yearned for.

More Than This.

Dark skies and cloudy days make it

difficult to see past this moment.

These years going in cyclical motions,

Never able to catch my

breath.

Around and around,

nothing wants to slow down.

Functioning in a mess bigger than me.

Trying to self sooth.

Two steps forward,

five steps back.

Decisions made for me, before me.

Unpacking bags that I never packed.

One arm extended towards hope,

Pulling in the opposite direction is the past.

Head to the sky,

"well God, is there any more than this?

…I'm Not a Kid Anymore

Back in the day, when I was young –

I'm not a kid anymore.

If I could go back to the days when I worried less because I didn't know as much. When I cared more, because I didn't know as much.

If I could go back to the days when I knew less, so, I didn't worry as much. When I felt so much, but really felt less.

If I could go back to the days when I thought this was worth living.

Back when I had hopes and dreams that felt like something that I could reach

No Love.

It's probably the tantalizing memory of her lying face down on the floor.

Black mascara staining the carpet,

Tears and –

Him who knows where?

This is love, I'm sure, because if it doesn't

hurt then he doesn't care. This must be love,

because even though last night he dragged her down the stairs by her hair,

the two of us watching knew the next morning she'd be there.

I know this is love because,

even though every night she's a slut, a whore and a bitch—

every morning with breakfast and gifts he convinces her, or –

She's convinced herself, there's no one else she'd rather be with.

And now that I know what love is, I don't want any parts of it.

Not even in the least bit.

Mrcme.

He found me in the last place I wanted to be found.

It was the eleventh hour.

Life was towering over me.

He brought light to that dark closet.

I had thrown in the towel,

Preparing to throw myself over the edge.

My soul was dead, and I

was trying to find the right moment to take my last breath.

Right at that moment He found me.

Wrapped me in his arms and saved me,

pulled me off the ledge, He gave me:

Forgiveness,

Provision and

Purpose to live in.

I thought I knew what I needed.

All those open wounds, He cleaned them.

And today He's showing me the newness to walk-in.

He saved me.

Forgiveness is freeing.

To **forgive** doesn't mean to forget—

it means you're taking back your **power.**

Forgive them and forgive yourself.

Reign.

Killing Me Softly (with this touch).

When mouths don't move things can still slide through the cracks, like predators sliding into bedrooms late night.

When you steal honest moments, it's like precious adolescence being stolen by the monster, in the closet.

They touch you and don't even know you.

That feeling is familiar.

Your intrusive nature reminds me of my aggressor.

Back then I didn't know to say stop, because my body betrayed me with a reaction of a go, and— today my no is a foreign concept apparently.

Too handsy and not even my man, see –

I understand you believe in casual sex, but my vagina is not the release for all your lost childhood screams.
Perhaps your mother should have hugged you more; maybe your father should have just stuck around.

Whatever the reason may be, I won't be your little whore.

You won't trump my private parts, because of the uncertainty of your masculinity.

Adding multiple bodies to your repertoire doesn't make you a man –more like a hoe.

Oh, and grabbing my tits without my permission really only makes you a bitch.

Them vs. Me (external conflict)

Sometimes I hate my body.

Really, I love it, but it does me no good.

All they ever want is my body,

As if my mind is no good.

Get my hopes up—

You're just hoping to lay me down,

Fondle me when no one else is around.

I was just a kid back then, and –

now I'm grown ass woman, tired of the only passion they have, being the kind that leaves me hating my body.

t.mac

Chilly Sunday nights hold cheap wine,

Good laughs and sweet memories.

As the music moves through the room,

I cannot help but remember the night we watched the stars, as I laid across your chest.

Effortless breaths accompanied by forehead kisses.

Tonight, along with many others,

I'm just hoping the feelings, with the memories are mutual.

Just My Type.

I'm done with smooth talkers.

Being a woman of many words-

They are my weakness.

Speaking so well, releases my meekness.

It makes me want to tear down this wall with my bare hands, and

hand them everything on the other side.

But they are never down to ride.

They just sing melodious lies.

Music to my ears.

But once the smoky mirrors clear,

I'm left high and dry.

Half the time without even a proper goodbye.

Eyes Wide Shut.

As a woman I should be able to say,

"I won't," – if you can't say,

"I do."

I hate that I'm always so willing to compromise me for what's not even the best of you.

You've gotten some of the best things I know about myself.

I have cared for you, shared my deepest regrets, and allowed your lies to run marathons around my heart.

Making me seemingly drunk.

I despise the things you've said

that were disguised as the truth.

The things that kept my moral conscience, aloof.

Bbygrl.P

Baby girl don't make that boy your world.

Don't let him dance and sing on your heart.

Trust God and be finished before it really starts.

It's never too late to take back your joy and guard your heart.

Smile again.

Make things right with God, your family and friends.

We've all been lost, but you're never too far.

There will never be too high a cost.

Jesus laid down his life, and

Surely one day he will make you someone's wife.

But, with time my love.
Love will find its way,
the beauty from the inside will shine and on that day your husband finds you, he will have found a good thing.

Thank God for your life, baby girl.

There is more to this life than what's in plain sight.

Don't let this boy take you from His light.

In this cold world let Him be your warmth, and

Let Him bring you the one who will show
and prove, just how real God's love is for you.

Secret Lovers. (nvrlettngo)

The whirlwind of emotions slowed just enough.

Just enough for me to pull myself up.

But disgust swarmed over me, and—

with too much shame and little hope,

I fell right back into something I should have never taken the time to know.

This Love Is… [blinding and binding]

I'd be a dummy to try again, but – if I do play stupid this time push me all the way in.

Don't let me teeter on both sides.

Remind me of all the sweet lies and say

them again.

Make them sweeter and more believable this time.

Suffocate *me* with the smoke for the mirrors.

I mean if we're going to do this, then we might as well go all the way this time.

Show me how much you haven't changed.

Hit me harder, and then we'll hit it harder – to

numb the pain.

Make my rivers of tears run into an ocean, this time.

I'll drown in the sorrows of lost yesterdays

and hopeless tomorrows, with you.

Torn and Scorned.

My pride got in the way.

Felt this coming,

Your demeanor gently demanded more, but

my pride got in the way.

Soft touches and sweet kisses are what you asked,

But I couldn't.

I once had all those handy tools,

the things a woman uses to

please, sometimes tease, and

really just keep her man.

They seem to be misplaced now or replaced with

harsh words and unforgettable degrading tones.

Yelling out,

"I knew you didn't deserve me!"

When my heart is really screaming,

"you hurt me."

Resistance.

Pushing and pulling.

Whatever he's doing, she's doing the opposite.

Playing on each other's hearts like a steady drum beat.

His heart beats faster when she's around, and

Sometimes he just needs her to be warm and welcoming.

But she's a cold bitch, naturally.

Find yourself, first.

Just don't be so desperate to have the love you lacked as a child,

That you shortchange yourself, by

settling as an adult.

I know about this because it was me, many times.

Wait on God, Trust

His timing,

and His will for your

life.

Not for NUN.

You start to wonder about yourself.

Like am I really only a hole and a couple balloons?

Am I always going to have to be the main act at the circus?

You start to wonder is it possible to want to be sexy, and

not be tried, every time, with the sex thing.

You start to wonder, should I just be a nun?

Because at this point, if that's what it takes then, suit me up and ship me out.

Maybe I am weird because all that sweet talk about the tease in my walk is, old to me, now.

(I mean) It's been a thing since I was barely thirteen.

(and) You mean to tell me I can't even use my God given strength to maneuver through life,

Without you using it as your sexual muse.

You mean to tell me that you've reduced the queen in me to peasantry, because—

you're not the king you claimed to be on IG.

My nigga you're weak.

[distant] Admiration.

Tell her she's beautiful and mean it,
without compromising who she is.
She's fragile in all the right ways—
at all the right times.
Yet, solid enough to take on life,
alone.
So, don't think she needs you for a thing.

Tell her she's beautiful and mean it,
without causing any part of her to be in your
shadow, unwillingly.
She's complete, and will not compete with the ego
of a man
that is secretly weak.
One who masked it long enough to get her, but
darkness is only for a time.
So, when the light shines, she realizes you never
had what it took to keep her.

Tell her she's beautiful, and just leave her.
You were merely a step along the way.
Maybe you needed to see something so rare, for
hope's sake.
But you can't keep her.

[not so] Invincible.

I took a shower when I made it in, but I'm still leaking.

And I did laundry immediately, but I'm still reeking.

Damn those burning incense.

Sitting here trying to figure out what happened.

How many times did I utter no, and—

How many times did you choose to hear go?

Right now, it's all a blur.

But I'm raw between my knees;

so, something happened

without consent.

Replaying the series of events,

what did I have on?

What did I say?

You'll say it was the pheromones.

I'd say you're a hazard zone.

No blinking lights,

No warning signs,

With no self-control.

Don't think I've ever heard myself sound so weak.

You'd be surprised who you become when you're forced to succumb to the insecurities of someone you thought you could trust.

You lay there breathing, but lifeless.

Maybe you always felt like a fighter, but

you don't know that you can fight this.

Don't want to hear anything, but you're frightened by the silence.

You have words,

but nothing can be said to right this.

[imbalanced] Adulting.

When life gets a hold of you, it shows. Suddenly

I've forgotten how to comb my hair.

No bodycons or dresses with a flair.

I've grown cold to social gatherings,

No friends around me.

Psyched myself out.

Made me believe this is who I am, and

this is who I want to be.

But, I remember who I used to be.

The person I was, before life tainted me,

tried to destroy me,

loved me then left me.

I begged for mercy, but life insists more pain.

And because you can't un-ring a bell,

Some days I'm reminded of the tragedies that changed me.

Randomly, mid laugh a flashback comes

just to say, "you're having too much fun,

  pipe down."

Me vs. Them

I can't even get a guy to make it into next week.

And it's not because of him, it's me.

Thought wooing and swooning was all I needed, but

Lately I'm more impressed with the things I've done for me.

In your current state,

I can't validate you anymore than you can satisfy me.

Be whole without me, because I'm one entirely.

I've already penetrated the infrastructure of hurt life built for me.

I've already purged the lies of who I'm supposed to be,

because of those who came before me.

I'm already prepared for what's coming-

seen and unseen.

[un] Clouded Thought:

When you're finally over hurt, it is—

liberating.

But the thing is, you must let yourself actually get over it.

Don't ignore it, try to numb it or try to force the end's hand.

Just feel every emotion and go through the journey.

A journey has a beginning middle and end.

So does your story.

Along the way you may double back, maybe even triple back. Don't be mad at yourself, though.

You are HUMAN. And it's true, the heart wants what the heart wants.

But at some point, you will have to look at

yourself and realize the truth AND accept it.

At some point your heart will have to want you more than them, or it or whatever it is that's hurting you.

Once you reach THAT point you've overcome.

I now realize the error in my ways
Self-love is to self-reflect.
Not to deflect your issues,
Not to ignore the truth in front of you-
or inside you,
or beside you.
If you love yourself, you'll never try to hide you.

i love me.

always take the time to reflect.

       learn from your mistakes,

       admit your wrongs-

              everything starts with you.

Sloane.

Whskeemepls

There's a lesson in the bottle,
I've yet to learn it, though.
This whiskey sliding down my throat,
releases the words I'd otherwise choke on.
Now I'm weighing the cons and the pros of
the last six months without him.
Counting the prose, I've written about him.
One shot turned into, three.
My homegirl said, "double it, it's on me."
Who am I to decline?

This Jack is helping me think.

Sweet Tooth.

and I'd do it again, because – this celibacy

thing isn't really working for me.

I never know if I'm going or coming.

Well, I know I'm not cumming,

Just don't know if I'm going to make it to marriage.

I basically shattered Pandora's box

Four years ago.

Found all the pieces, glued them back together, and

I became a perfectly jagged piece of art.

An oxymoron.

Then stupidly tapped in again

one year ago,

but he didn't even have a big enough ego, to

make it worth it.

You ever heard of a milk chocolate sucker?

It sucks not being able to self sooth, or

Suck 'til you ooze.

I remember one night; it was

the fresh start to a week.

Why not get him weak?

Drinks with my bestie turned into a mess with a quick text.

One thing led to another, and

Much obliged, he returned my kindness with kisses.

He missed his ole lady, and – I missed my hard-caramel candy. Now fast forward two years, and I don't know how to subdue the urges.

Some days I want love.

On others, I salivate for one of those suckers:

Caramel, milk chocolate, dark chocolate, it doesn't matter.

Just let me satisfy this sweet tooth, soon.

Baby Bye.

Your grip speaks of your insecurities.

Holding him that tight doesn't mean that by the end of the night, he won't be inquiring about me.

But let's be clear, I don't want your man.

Whether or not he's yours,

isn't dependent on how tight you hold his arm, it's up to him.

So, stop side eyeing every woman that walks

by,

because your guy has a wandering eye.

Computer Love

Reason number seven hundred forty-three why these times we live in aren't for me.

Just last week my mom tried to convince me to find my love virtually.

But I know that's not for me.

Dial my number, don't send me a tweet.

Let's engage each other mentally.

Follow each other through the park.

Leave marks on each other's hearts.

Not to be confused with a comment left on a Facebook post.

I'm intrigued the most by,

the similarities in our disdain for modern technology.

Bottom of My Glass

Feels like I just ordered this drink.

Now I'm thinking about who to call, and at

this hour, what will they think?

Matter of fact, forget that let me scroll through my recents.

Jamaal it is, and hopefully he answers,

because I'd rather him, than Terry.

Damn you rum and coke,

Why must I meet your end so quickly?

Candid Conversations.

Learning that love isn't necessarily the infatuation of them being too good to be true, or not being able to take my eyes off you.
Maybe more like I got you when you are down to your last two.
Living in this fictional reality.
Polluted conversations doused in sweet red wine, Deep sighs at the good times and cries of why.
Probably could be in love by now if it wasn't for Tony or Terry or Quentin.
Nah I could have been in love by now if it wasn't for me.
Wait, what's the definition of insanity?
It's listening to all the same 90's R&B jams cyclically, expecting them to come true.
I'm writing four-page letters to niggas that: don't read, can't read or just chose not to.
It's 2017, and I'm sounding a lot like Monica and Brandy.
Coming across more scrubs than TLC.
Sitting up in my room, tryna figure out how, my ex is still a factor, because Ms. Lauryn I haven't experienced reciprocity since—
well never.

A damsel in distress, at this cliff.
When you jump will you fall, or will you glide?
Pondering your next move thinking,
"but what if?
What if I crash and burn?"
Oh, but queen what if you fly?

[Don't] Text Me.

I might leave that shit on read.
Maybe you're dead to me,
but maybe I'm still hurt.
You should have made us work,
because nothing I did worked.
These text messages tell it all.
But, if you give me the chance,
I'll find a new reason to fall.

All 2018

Reclaiming my time.

Giving him back every heart felt lie.

I'm all out of tries, and

just when I'm getting back to me, he has the audacity to

want to see if we could – "try again",

Make amends,

be friends.

Funny how things go out of style, then

come back in.

You're following the trends.

Well, when will treating a queen as such come back around?

Doesn't really matter, because by the time you catch on

I'll be halfway down somebody's aisle.

*Kanye shrugg.

Every Once in a While.

Really, I just need to be rubbed on.

My scalp,

My ear,

My fingers,

Hell, even my feet, and

I don't even like feet,

My butt,

My heart,

My legs…

My throat with your tongue.

Us Together.

dim lights.
two bodies.
scattered thoughts.
throbbing. perspiring.
fully compromising.
can't lie
it's everything.
nothing matters.
time passing.
reality settling.
from you,
to me.
beard game,
so right.
my eyes.
your hands.
this music.
only tonight.

Only with You.

exchanging needs for wants.
abandoning every moral
thought. compromising all
self-value.
Loving every minute of it.

But Tonight...

Removing the make-up.

Disassembling the layers of clothes.

Over time she's grown fond of *herself*.

Tonight, as the mirror stands innocently in front of her naked body,

it's like she's never seen anything more beautiful.

Mesmerized by her own silky brown skin.

She never found much beauty in it before,

But tonight, showed her something different.

Release.

Tonight, I want to occupy my floorspace.
Lay here aimlessly and stretch.
Maybe draft a new poem.

I love the rush that comes when my pen is stroking
the paper, getting my poetic juices flowing.
I'm always amazed at my performance, when I go
back to read it.

But tonight, it's not the same—
writer's block.
Biting down on my lip and sucking the excess
saliva.
There seems to be no climax in
sight.
So, I flip the page and start over.
Coming from a different angle,
now, I'm at a steady pace.

Wishful Thinking.

I opened the doors for communication.

So, of course you waltz right through them.

But how does one explain that it was the Remy talking, and

I don't want to cause confusion, but that broad is more daring than,

Whiskey.

Two years in and things are still kinda tricky.

Playing like I'm not tryna play for keeps.

Like my heart didn't just sink, when you answered the phone.

Partially because I miss you,

and then because I know he ain't you.

Man, what a way to wishfully drink.

Do You?

Wait, do you have a girlfriend?

I only ask because a lot of times, almost immediately,

that information is omitted from the conversation.

So, before we explore mental stimulation,

I need to know.

Spare Me.

I be needing closure, but

I don't be wanting to hear my conscience taunt me with that godawful,

"I told you so."

Ready.

I'm not dippin' back this time.

If I do, I'll be salty, like Lot's wife.

See, I know now that God's not playing with me.

And yes, what's for me is for me; so, I

can't miss my own beat.

But,

blessings have been delayed, one too many times for my liking.

It's time out for the dudes that can only like, because

God knows, I need love.

[Looking for better] Communication Skills

Now I'm sitting here stressed out,
Ready to leave. Feels like I've
missed my beat.
like my dignity has a bad leak.
My confidence is oozing out, but this
feeling is so me.
Not knowing what to say initially.
Leading me to underthink and over speak.
Projectile saying shit I don't even mean.
"Damn girl, why are you so mean?"
Really, I'm not though, but
How do you convince him of that when his
confidence is now shot?
Like, how do you go from,
"we can never be." to "I can see a future for you and
me,"
all in one week.
I'm indecisive, but so are you.
Bear with me, though.
Hear me out, stay with me and don't
leave without, giving us a fair chance.

Balance Is...

Having the urge to tell you I love you all day, but settling for a periodic, "You ok?" Because you need to unplug.

Plus, we're just friends anyway.

The Jones is Gone.

I hope you don't wake up one morning, ten years from now,

Thinking maybe it was her.

Hopefully those kisses never become bitter,

making you remember how sweet mine were.

I hope the laughs never become shallow,

the conversations hollow or the love frugal,

because I'll be sending you a four-page letter,

and it will read:

"I told you so," in as many different ways possible.

"I told you that

nobody would ever love you quite like me,

 rub you the right way quite like me,

think of you the way I do,

pray for you, or

catch flights and reach new heights in life with you,

the way I do."

The Jones is Gone.

I hope you don't wake up one morning, ten years from now,

Thinking maybe it was her.

Hopefully those kisses never become bitter,

making you remember how sweet mine were.

I hope the laughs never become shallow,

the conversations hollow or the love frugal,

because I'll be sending you a four-page letter,

and it will read:

"I told you so," in as many different ways possible.

"I told you that

nobody would ever love you quite like me,

 rub you the right way quite like me,

think of you the way I do,

pray for you, or

catch flights and reach new heights in life with you,

the way I do."

Balance Is...

Having the urge to tell you I love you all day, but settling for a periodic, "You ok?" Because you need to unplug.
Plus, we're just friends anyway.

Circa Spring 2016

Don't let these memories be in vain.

Never forget the nights that we spread our wings, and flew, like the love birds were.

There was nothing better than the feeling of drawing near to you in public.

Surrounded by people, but only seeing you.

That night,

Frenchman Street felt like it belonged to you and me.

The lights in the courtyard were so bright;

they illuminated the love in my heart for you.

Please don't ever downplay that night or your

love for me.

Never make me seem like just another girl on the list.

Like the passion in our kiss didn't exist, or

like it didn't tell you exactly what we could

be.

Don't ever act like you didn't consider forever with me,

But you didn't have the audacity to let us be.

The Strongest Drug I've Ever Known

So toxic, but

I itched for that scent

So toxic, but

My body craved it

So toxic, but

there wasn't a thing I wouldn't do to have it.

A fiend is something I never thought I'd be,

but in my sleep, I never dreamed I'd get my hands on anything as potent as you.

Like the purest cocaine,

five straight white lines.

Your touch

Your smile

Your hugs

Our fights

Our lies

Could we get much higher than this?

Purple and blue you left my wrist.

Numbing every ounce of emotion, which

silenced all moral thoughts.

My ears yearned for the deafening heights your voice reached, as we argued about why she was texting you so late.

Confusing love and hate
I hated you, but my condition kept
me in restraints.
Even when I wanted to leave, I stayed.
No rehab could fix the damage done by this drug called our love.

Clouded Thought:

He doesn't know what love is, and he doesn't know how to respond to this. I'm not saying it's quite love, yet. But I'm saying if it were, he couldn't handle it. Life has conditioned him to play the game, and play it well.

Aaand Cut.

I hate you because,

everything I tried to prevent you from being,

is everything you fought to be.

My latest rendition of the "man for me".

Not that you even believed this could be anything more than the nothing you intended.

Woe is me.

Once again, his only objective is to take me down, piece-by-piece.

I hate you because every moment I felt like I

needed you, the most, were the moments you were

doing me dirty.

When I wished your legs were intertwined in mine,

she was taking my place.

When I felt I wanted to tell you my

hurt, you were elsewhere— sexing

yours away.

Doubt.

Can you not always set in so quickly,

making everything seem so deceiving.

Can you not come until we call for you next time?

I wasn't ready to turn in my laughter,

the butterflies weren't done playing, and

I wasn't ready for the frustration of the morning after.

When Did I Get So Emotional?

When you made my mind wonder?

The mystery in your stride.

Speaking very little and looking

so passionately.

With the first lie?

Wanted to call, but I didn't.

Time passed and before you, I was again.

With a gentle approach you didn't let the day end without confirmation.

When you let me into your space?

Making moves every which way.

You made me comfortable with your touch.

When you guided me through your mind?

Sitting across from one another, playing

each moment over and over.

(Silently) hoping and praying.

When your actions exceeded my expectations?

Head to chest, legs intertwined.

Holding my waist tight, along
with my mind.

I got emotional *when I felt like you should be my man,*

but quickly realized you'd never be.

Taxicab Confessions...

I am not drunk sir.

I live up the street; I could have walked, but—

I need to talk.

And I just need you to listen.

That boy played me sir.

He played me.

Unequally yoked, so

I know that lifestyle was a sin, but

I was all in.

We equally indulged, that night.

The morning after was like nothing even happened.

He didn't even mention it.

But I did put him to sleep.

Sir, I'm not drunk, but can you take the scenic route?

I just want to see if he's out.

He told me he couldn't join me for drinks tonight.

Claims, "too much work."

Oooh, cut that up, sir!

"work, work, work, work, work, work, work!"

That's my jam!

We danced to this in a reggae club down south.

Those were some good times.

Why didn't he mention it sir?

He left me to my own devices.

"5231 South Drexel, maam—

wake up,

Ma'am, we have arrived at your place."

Oh, thank you sir, Thanks for everything.

Taxicab Conversations...

Good evening sir,

Recently, I visited Little Haiti and

those people were beautiful.

I like the way their skin glows— dewy

almost exactly how the people in New Orleans are kissed by the sun, and

wrapped in the cool breeze of a moonlit summer night.

Sir, I'm a city girl, but those southern men do something to me.

This one guy looked so scrumptious,

I thought about undressing him right in the middle of the beach.

The stillness of the south is so soothing, but would drive me crazy, simultaneously.

Up here my thoughts are drowned out by city traffic,

Sirens and other people's outbursts of drama.

Down there I am alone with my madness.

Sir, and those men down south take care of you.

I am thinking of relocating,

maybe to Atlanta—

the black mecca, or Texas.

I need a change and a man.

Chicago isn't quite doing it for me, but

it's not time to go to D.C.

You know what let me out right here.

I'll walk the rest of the way.

I need to think.

I don't trust new people with the old me.
So, I keep it all in.
Rewind, fast forward, replaying it all in my head.
I'm kind of going crazy trying to seem sane-
Keeping everybody at bay.

help me.

Clouded Thought:

Maybe I'm everything they say I am:

Mean, angry, bitter, aggressive,

But then again, may I'm the truth they just can't face.

Love yourself the way you need to be loved.

Stop looking for others to do something, for you, that you won't do for yourself.

About the Author:

Hi, I'm Portia D—a writer from Bolingbrook, IL. 'Nightmares and Daydreams' came about as a mental release while pursuing my undergraduate degree. And aside from all the formal things this is probably supposed to include, I just want to say that I'm just an ordinary girl, with real life experiences; but through the grace of God, I can enjoy life, dream and watch my dreams come into fruition. Thank you, a million times for supporting.

-xo

I hope you enjoyed.

www.ingramcontent.com/pod-product-compliance
Lightning Source LLC
Chambersburg PA
CBHW021446080526
44588CB00009B/720